Life of Fred®

Begin Teaching

Life of Fred®
Begin Teaching

Stanley F. Schmidt, Ph.D.

Polka Dot Publishing

ISBN: 978-1-937032-14-2

Printed and bound in the United States of America

Polka Dot Publishing   Reno, Nevada

To order copies of books in the Life of Fred series,

visit our website PolkaDotPublishing.com

Questions or comments? Email the author at lifeoffred@yahoo.com

First printing

Life of Fred®:Begin Teaching was illustrated by the author with additional clip art furnished under license from Nova Development Corporation, which holds the copyright to that art.

for Goodness' sake

or as J.S. Bach—who was
never noted for his plain
English—often expressed it:

Ad Majorem Dei Gloriam
(to the greater glory of God)

If you happen to spot an error that the author, the publisher, and the printer missed, please let us know with an email to: lifeoffred@yahoo.com

SPECIAL OFFER

As a reward, we'll email back to you a list of all the corrections that readers have reported.

A Note Before We Begin

This is the second book in the Life of Fred® language arts series. These language arts books will cover English from every angle.

In this volume, we will learn about the adventures of Fred from late afternoon on Tuesday until 9 a.m. on Wednesday. Even though Fred is only five years old, the readers of his adventures may/might/should be a little older.

By the end of this book you will be able to answer:

❀ What is the past perfect progressive form of the verb *to sing*?
❀ What are the five ways to pronounce the letter *a*?
❀ What are the meanings of the verbs *affect* and *effect*?
❀ What are the meanings of the nouns *affect* and *effect*?
❀ What are the 16 ways to create plurals in English?
❀ What does it mean to read *Moby Dick* at a deeper level than just as a fishing story?
❀ What is the rule for verbs in which the compound subjects are connected by *or*? The hats or the coat is/are mine.
❀ How can you define a consonant in terms of air flow, instead of just saying that it isn't a vowel?
❀ Why is it silly to put anapestic on an iambic foot?
. . . and many more topics in language arts.

AND MORE

There is an essential body of knowledge that every well-educated person should have. English is important.

English!

Math is important. But so are many other areas of learning. There is no reason why each subject should be kept in water-tight compartments. They flow together naturally.

In this book you will learn:
❀ why you can't buy a kangaroo at your local pet store
❀ where Tasmania is located
❀ how Russian has three numbers when English only has two (singular and plural)
❀ how to sing the "Alpha, Beta, Gamma, Delta, Epsilon" song (The sheet music is included in this book.)

HOW THIS BOOK IS ORGANIZED

Each chapter is a daily lesson. There are about four pages of reading about the adventures of Fred and a Your Turn to Play.

Have a paper and pencil handy before you sit down to read.

Each Your Turn to Play consists of about three or four questions. Write out the answers—don't just orally answer them.

After all the questions are answered, then take a peek at my answers that are given on the next page.

Don't just read the questions and look at the answers. You won't learn as much that way.

A NOTE FROM STAN

Fred spends some exciting and some anxious moments getting ready to Begin Teaching a new subject (English) in a new country (Australia).

Almost every teacher experiences some of those feelings at the beginning of a new school year.

By the time that Fred finsihed his first hour of teaching, which is at the end of this book, he was feeling good again.

Contents

Chapter One
Meeting Mack

Mack

Fred was so happy to have found Mack. Together they hopped into Mack's car and headed to the Board of Missions office.

On Sunday Fred had written to the Board of Missions, "I want to be a friend, help people in trouble . . . I do love to teach."*

Now, two days later, Fred was in Australia heading to the board office in Wagga Wagga. He was eager to begin teaching. He had taught math at KITTENS University for five years, and he knew he could teach any math course that was needed. It was June 4. He was going to spend the whole summer in Australia. He had never been outside the United States before. When Fred sat in Mack's car, he couldn't see anything except the sky. He was too short.

Fred is there, but you can't see him.

---

*The three dots (. . .) are called an **ellipsis** (ee-LIP-sis). An ellipsis indicates something has been left out. In Fred's letter he had written, *"I want to be a friend, help people in trouble, teach, dig a well to get clean water, and kill mosquitos. I don't know how to dig a well or kill mosquitos, but I do love to teach."*

Fred couldn't find any seatbelts. Fred thought *This must be a really old car.*

Mack said, "This car is not brand new."

Time Out!

Both Fred and Mack said the same thing. Mack's way of saying it is called an understatement.

Understatements:

Oceans have some water in them.

Being run over by a car is irritating.

Understatements with "not":

This car is not brand new.

Fred is not extremely tall.

Having a pizza, a milkshake, and a piece of pie for lunch is not a starvation diet.

Understatements with "not" in them have a special name. They are called litotes. (LIE-toe-tease)

When someone learns that he has just won a million dollars, he might say, "That ain't bad." That's litotes.

Mack said, "The Mission Board here in Wagga Wagga does not have a lot a money (litotes). This car may be old, but it still runs. We are so happy that people like you, Fred, would volunteer to come and help."

"I'm too small to help dig wells," Fred said. "But I'm not bad at teaching (litotes)."

Mack was a little confused. He was told to pick up a famous college professor from KITTENS University. He was also told that Fred Gauss had been teaching there for five years and had won many teaching awards.

Mack said, "You mention being small. Looking at you, some people might think that you were just a child rather than a man who is very short. You are about a meter tall."

"Not quite," Fred said. "A meter is about 39 inches. I'm 36 inches tall, which is one yard."

Mack said, "I like your bow tie. That makes you look older. Have you ever thought of growing a beard? Then people wouldn't mistake you for a child."

Mack didn't know that he was talking to a five-year-old.

They arrived. Mack got out of the car. Fred reached down to unfasten (silent *t*) his seatbelt and then realized he hadn't been wearing one. Fred realized that if Mack had crashed the car, he might have been thrown through the windshield.*

––––––––––––––––––––

* Have you ever noticed that there are no seatbelts on motorcycles?

Fred had imagined that the Wagga Wagga office building of the Board of Missions would look very fancy.

How Fred pictured it

He knew they were doing important work: helping people in trouble, digging wells to get clean water, teaching, and killing mosquitos. What he didn't realize was that the work was the important thing—not making a big name for itself.

Every member of the Board had received this memo:

Notice
to All Board Members

Our job is to love people. It's that simple.

Do that without showing off. Don't go around bragging. No special titles for any of you.

Give them h's:

Hold the hand of those who are crying.

Help the poor.

Heal the sick.

Wait a minute! I, your reader, have a question.[*]

What did you have in mind?

There's an English error in that notice. In the previous book you told us the eight ways to make something plural.

1. one cat → two cats	– → s
2. one calf → two calves	f → ves
3. one foot → two feet	irregular plurals
4. one deer → two deer	no change
5. one toss → two tosses	s → es
6. one mystery → two mysteries	y → ies
7. one hippopotamus → two hippopotami	us → i
8. one alumna → two alumnae	a → ae

In this "Notice to All Board Members," the plural of h was h's. That's not any of the eight ways to make a plural.

You are right. That's the ninth way to make a plural. Lower case (uncapitalized) letters are special. There are seven *e*'s in the previous sentence.

Your Turn to Play

Write your answers down before looking at my answers.

If you don't remember the spelling, turn to earlier pages to find it.

1. (Fill in the blank) "This Your Turn to Play is not very long" is an example of _____.

2. (Fill in the blank) A, B, C, D, . . . , X, Y, Z uses an _____.

---

[*] Life of Fred books are the only books in the world in which the reader can talk back to the author.

·······**ANSWERS**·······

1. "This Your Turn to Play is not very long" is an example of litotes .

    Instead of saying it was not very long, you could have said that it was short.

2. A, B, C, D, . . . , X, Y, Z uses an ellipsis .

small essay

Sometimes English Makes Sense

I can't tell you why yacht is spelled y-a-c-h-t.

I can't tell you why the plural of die is dice.

yacht

die

dice

But I do have a guess as to why we use an apostrophe to make the plurals of lower case letters. If we didn't use an apostrophe, then I might write, "There are eight as you can see in the previous sentence."

If we use the apostrophe, the sentence becomes clear: "There are eight a's you can see in the previous sentence."

end of small essay

18

Chapter Two
Teachers Quit

The office of the Board of Missions in Wagga Wagga wasn't a fancy building with high rent. They shared an old building with a junk store. The rent was very cheap.

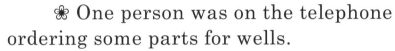

Mack and Fred headed inside.

❀ One person was on the telephone ordering some parts for wells.

❀ Two people were putting cans of food in boxes for hungry families.

Mack wanted to introduce Fred to Sylvia. She was in charge of the teaching assignments for Australia. As they walked over to her desk, Mack told Fred, "Since we heard that you were coming here to teach, three of our teachers have quit."

Sylvia

Fred was stunned. He didn't know what to think. He wondered *Why did all those teachers quit just because I was coming here to teach?*

Sylvia turned to Fred and smiled. She asked, "Why are you crying little boy? Are you hungry? Did you lose your parents?"

"I made three of your teachers quit," Fred sobbed. "I'm sorry. If I had known that, I wouldn't have volunteered to come here."

Sylvia was confused.

Mack explained, "This is Professor Fred Gauss. He's the one that Jennifer, the board chairman, said would be coming today."

Sylvia could tell the difference between a boy and a very short man. She asked him, "How old are you, Fred?"

Fred dried his tears with his handkerchief and said, "Five. Why did all those people quit just because I was coming to help?"

Sylvia asked Mack, "Do you know what he's talking about?"

Mack shrugged his shoulders. "All I told him was that we had three teachers quit in the last couple of days."

Fred looked up and said, "Huh?"

small essay

The Dangerous Word *Since*

Mack had said, "Since we heard that you were coming here, three of our teachers have quit."

What Fred understood was, "*Because* we heard that you were coming, three of our teachers quit."

What Mack meant was, "*Since the time* we heard you were coming, three of our teachers quit."

The word *since* has two different meanings.

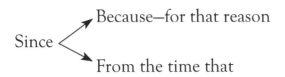

The whole point of English is to communicate clearly.
The whole point of English is to communicate clearly.
The whole point of English is to communicate clearly.
The whole point of English is to communicate clearly.
The whole point of English is to communicate clearly.

Mack wasn't communicating clearly when he said, "Since we heard that you were coming here, three of our teachers quit."

end of small essay

Sylvia gave Fred a big hug and told him that they were glad he was here. She explained to him that one of the teachers had to quit because she was expecting a baby soon. One of them was retiring after teaching for 42 years. The third one had been drafted into the army.

"So you can see," Sylvia said, "we really need your help. Today is Tuesday, June 4. How soon can you start?"

Fred looked at the clock on the wall. It was 20 minutes after five.

5:20

21

He said, "Could you give me ten minutes? I could start at 5:30."

Sylvia did not expect that answer. Most people would have said something like, "Would next Monday be okay?" They would need time to unpack and prepare some lesson plans.

Fred didn't need any time to unpack. He had seven dollars in his pocket and no luggage.

He didn't need any time to prepare lessons for teaching any math subject. He had taught math at KITTENS University for five years. He could teach the Green's Theorem in Space[*] as easily as teaching 3 + 4 = 7.

Sylvia said, "Our classes run from eight in the morning until five in the afternoon. Those three teachers that had to quit split up those nine hours[**] among themselves. How many hours each day would you like to teach?"

---

[*] Green's Theorem in Space, also known as the Divergence Theorem says

$$\oiint \mathbf{F} \cdot \mathbf{n} \, dS = \iiint (M_x + N_y + P_z) \, dV \text{ where}$$

$\mathbf{F}(x, y, z) = M(x, y, z)\mathbf{i} + N(x, y, z)\mathbf{j} + P(x, y, z)\mathbf{k}$ and $\mathbf{n}$ is a unit normal to some closed surface. This is one of the hardest theorems in fourth semester college calculus. It is a lot easier once you have had two years of algebra, a year of high school geometry, trig, and three semesters of calculus.

[**] From 8 a.m. to noon is four hours. From noon to 5 p.m. is five hours.

Fred made a little poem, "Nine would be fine." He had been teaching nine hours per day for years at KITTENS University.

Fred didn't realize *what* he would be teaching here in Australia.

Schedule
8–9 Beginning Algebra
9–10 Advanced Algebra
10–11 Geometry
11–noon Trigonometry
noon–1 Calculus
1–2 Statistics
2–3 Linear Algebra
3–3:05 Break
3:05–5 Seminar in Biology, Economics, Physics, Set Theory, Topology, and Metamathematics

Fred's university schedule

Your Turn to Play

1. What are the silent letters in each of these words?

    knife

    people

    soften

2. The rule for writing the plural of a word ending in *y* is

    ❖ y → ys if the letter before the *y* is a vowel (*a, e, i, o,* or *u*)

    ❖ y → ies if the letter before the *y* is not a vowel

    Write the plurals of:

    story

    city

    toy

    body

    boy

    day

```
┌─────────────────────────────────────────────────────────┐
```

. . . . . . .COMPLETE SOLUTIONS . . . .

1.   *knife*   The *k* is silent.

      people   The *o* is silent.

      soften   The *t* is silent.

2.   *story* → stories   (*r* is not a vowel.)

      city → cities   (*t* is not a vowel.)

      toy → toys   (*o* is a vowel.)

      body → bodies   (*d* is not a vowel)

      boy → boys   (*o* is a vowel)

      day → days   (*a* is a vowel)

```
└─────────────────────────────────────────────────────────┘
```

Sometimes English makes sense. If there is a vowel before the *y* and you replaced the *y* with *ies,* you could get some pretty weird looking words. boy → boies. There would be three vowels in a row.

The vowels: aeiou.

The letters that are not vowels: bcdfghjklmnpqrstvwxyz.

The letters that are not vowels are called **consonants**.

Vowels and Consonants for Adults

It all has to do with air flow from the lungs. Vowels have smooth air flow. Consonants mess with the air flow one way or another.

Some consonants block the flow: p, b, t, d, k, and g.

Some consonants divert the flow: m, n, and ng send the air through the nose.

Some consonants slow the flow: f, v, s, and z.

In some words, y and w, act as vowels, for example, the y in style.

Singing teachers tell their students to sing on the vowels. You can't sing a consonant and make it sound pretty.

Chapter Three
Today

Sylvia was delighted that Fred was willing to teach nine hours each day. She said the classroom is in Dubbo.

Dah-Who?

Fred had never heard of Dubbo. He didn't know whether it was a neighborhood in Wagga Wagga or some distance part of Australia.

"I will drive you there," Sylvia said. Then she added, "I tell you today you shall be with me in Dubbo."

❁   ❁   ❁

Time out!

The whole point of English is to communicate clearly.
The whole point of English is to communicate clearly.
The whole point of English is to communicate clearly.
The whole point of English is to communicate clearly.
The whole point of English is to communicate clearly.

There are two different meanings to the words: *I tell you today you shall be with me in Dubbo.*

Meaning #1: *I tell you today, you shall be with me in Dubbo.* Translation: Today I'm telling you that we will be together in Dubbo.

Meaning #2: *I tell you, today you shall be with me in Dubbo.* Translation: We are going to get there today.

The big difference is where you put the comma.

I tell you today, you shall be with me in Dubbo.

I tell you, today you shall be with me in Dubbo.

Commas can change the meaning.

❁   ❁   ❁

Sylvia pointed to a map on the wall. It showed the southeast (down right) part of Australia.

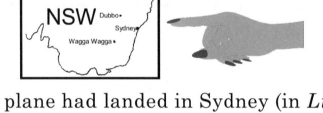

Fred's plane had landed in Sydney (in *Life of Fred: Australia*). Wagga Wagga was where the Board of Missions office was located. He found Dubbo on the map.

He asked Sylvia, "If this is the southeast part of Australia, why is it labeled North-South-West?"

Sylvia said, "That's a common mistake. NSW doesn't stand for North-South-West. It means New South Wales. Toowoomba is in the part of Australia called Queensland."

Toowoomba is mentioned ten times in *Life of Fred: Geometry*.

"Well, let's get going," Sylvia said. "It's going to take several hours to get to Dubbo."

They climbed in the same car that Mack had used. By sharing one car, the office cut down expenses.

Mack said Sylvia looked a little tired.* She had been working from 5 a.m. It was now 5 p.m. That was twelve hours.** Sylvia liked to say, "I work half-time. Twelve hours out of 24."

It was starting to get dark. June, July, and August are the cold, dark months of the year in Wagga Wagga. In June the average high temperature is only 14°.***

(Author's note: I'd love to put a fourth footnote on this page, but it won't fit. That might set a world's record for footnotes on a page.)

_____

* Of course, if we add a couple of commas, the meaning of the sentence changes completely: *Mack, said Sylvia, looked a little tired.* Now it would be Mack who would be tired.

** From 5 a.m. to noon is 7 hours. From noon to 5 p.m. is 5 hours. 7 + 5 = 12.

*** In Australia they use the metric system. Temperature is measured in Celsius, not in Fahrenheit. 14°C = 57°F. There is only one major country in the world that doesn't use metric. It lies between Canada and Mexico.

They headed on the Olympic Highway. Then on State Route 85, looking for signs for Temora. After 88 kilometers (= 57 miles) she turned onto Goldfields Way.

"I'm getting hungry," Sylvia said.

Fred expected that they would stop at some fast food place. He was preparing to tell her that he wasn't very hungry.

Sylvia surprised him when she said, "Would you climb in the backseat and fetch the basket?"

Fred had never climbed around in a car. He had also never been in a car without seatbelts. (Most cars in Australia have seatbelts.) He found the basket and brought it back to the front seat.

Sylvia reached in and took a turkey sandwich and a bottle of apple juice. She invited Fred to help himself.

Ever polite, Fred said, "Thank you," but he was more sleepy than hungry. It was dark outside now. He was getting ready to head off to the Land of Nod. Fred had done a lot of traveling since Sunday.

Your Turn to Play

1. The last sentence on the previous page was, "Fred had done a lot of traveling since Sunday." It used the word *since*.

Does this sentence have a single meaning or is the sentence ambiguous? (am-BIG-you-us ambiguous = has more than one possible meaning)

2. Name three countries in the world that use the metric system.

3. Travis was one of the three teachers that quit. He used to drive the office car on Wednesdays. Which of these three is correct?

   A. Wednesday was Travis's day to drive.

   B. Wednesday was Travis' day to drive.

   C. Wednesday was Travises day to drive.

4. Which is these is correct?
     of

   A. "Wednesday is my day" said Travis.

   B. "Wednesday is my day", said Travis.

   C. "Wednesday is my day," said Travis.

. . . . ANSWERS . . . .

1. There are two possible meanings for the word *since*: (1) because or (2) from that time.

In the sentence *Fred had done a lot of traveling since Sunday,* only one of those meanings makes sense. The sentence has only one meaning. It is not ambiguous.

(*Since* and *sense* are homonyms.)

2. This is an easy question if you can name any three countries other than the United States.

There are three countries that haven't switched over to the metric system: United States, Liberia, and Myanmar.

Here are some of the countries that have gone metric: Afghanistan, Albania, Algeria, Andorra, Angola, Antigua and Barbuda, Argentina, Armenia, Australia, Austria, Azerbaijan, The Bahamas, Bahrain, Bangladesh, Barbados, Belarus, Belgium, Belize, Benin, Bhutan, Bolivia, Bosnia and Herzegovina, Botswana, Brazil, Brunei, Bulgaria, Burkina Faso, Burundi, Cambodia, Cameroon, Canada, Cape Verde, Central African Republic, Chad, Chile, China, Colombia, Comoros, Costa Rica, Cote d'Ivoire, Croatia, Cuba, Cyprus, Czech Republic, Denmark, Djibouti, Dominica, Dominican Republic, East Timor, Ecuador, Egypt, El Salvador, Equatorial Guinea, Eritrea, Estonia, Ethiopia, Fiji, Finland, France, Gabon, The Gambia, Georgia, Germany, Ghana, Greece, Grenada, Guatemala, Guinea, Guinea-Bissau, Guyana, Haiti, Honduras, Hungary, Iceland, India, Indonesia, Iran, Iraq, Ireland, Israel, Italy, Jamaica, Japan, Jordan, Kazakhstan, Kenya, Kiribati, Korea, North, Korea, South, Kosovo, Kuwait, Kyrgyzstan, Laos, Latvia, Lebanon, Lesotho, Libya, Liechtenstein, Lithuania, Luxembourg, Macedonia, Madagascar, Malawi, Malaysia, Maldives, Mali, Malta, Marshall Islands, Mauritania, Mauritius, Mexico, Micronesia, Federated States of, Moldova, Monaco, Mongolia, Montenegro, Morocco, Mozambique, Namibia, Nauru, Nepal, Netherlands, New Zealand, Nicaragua, Niger, Nigeria, Norway, Oman, Pakistan, Palau, Panama, Papua New Guinea, Paraguay, Peru, Philippines, Poland, Portugal, Qatar, Romania, Russia, Rwanda, Saint Kitts and Nevis, Saint Lucia, Saint Vincent and the Grenadines, Samoa, San Marino, Sao Tome and Principe, Saudi Arabia, Senegal, Serbia, Seychelles, Sierra Leone, Singapore, Slovakia, Slovenia, Solomon Islands, Somalia, South Africa, Spain, Sri Lanka, Sudan, Suriname, Swaziland, Sweden, Switzerland, Syria, Taiwan, Tajikistan, Tanzania, Thailand, Togo, Tonga, Trinidad and Tobago, Tunisia, Turkey, Turkmenistan, Tuvalu, Uganda, Ukraine, United Arab Emirates, United Kingdom, Uruguay, Uzbekistan, Vanuatu, Vatican City, Venezuela, Vietnam, Yemen, Zambia, and Zimbabwe.

3. A. Wednesday was Travis's day to drive. You only use the apostrophe and no *s* when the original word is both plural and already ends in *s,* for example, the states' capitals.

4. C. "Wednesday is my day," said Travis. Commas come before close quotes.

Chapter Four
Arrival at Night

Sylvia turned right onto Newell Highway. After a couple hundred kilometers she turned onto Golden Highway. At 9:30 p.m. they got to Dubbo.

Fred had been snoozing for most of the trip. Every once in a while he would open his eyes and notice that it was still dark. He would shut his eyes and the sound of the car heading down the highway would send him off to sleep again.

He would need all the sleep he could get. Tomorrow would be Wednesday, June 5. He would be teaching for nine hours to students he had never seen, in a classroom he had never been in.

"Wake up, sleepyhead," Sylvia said gently. "We've arrived."

Fred was half awake. She picked him up and carried him to his home where he would spend the summer. She was surprised at how light he was (37 pounds).

The street lights cast a shadow from the school toward his house.

Fred's house for the summer

She carried him inside and laid him in his
bed. As he lay there half asleep,
she told him, "I've got to head
back to Wagga Wagga tonight.

Tomorrow morning I meet the
man who will be heading to
Tasmania for mosquito
abatement.* I hope you have a
wonderful summer teaching
English. Goodnight."

After Sylvia shut the door, he suddenly
realized what she had said. He sat up in bed.
She had said, "I hope you have a wonderful
summer teaching English."

Fred thought to himself, *I
have taught math for five years
at KITTENS University. I've never taught
English.*

He was sure that he had mentioned
mathematics in the letter he had sent to the
Board of Missions. He had kept a copy of that
letter.

He pulled it out of his pocket and read it:

---

* a-BAIT-ment (with the *a* like the *a* in alone) To abate
something is to lessen, to diminish.

June 2

Dear Friends at the Board of Missions,

On the coloring sheet you wrote, "Please write to us." I am writing to you.

I want to be a friend, help people in trouble, teach, dig a well to get clean water, and kill mosquitos.

I don't know how to dig a well or kill mosquitos, but I do love to teach. I have been teaching at KITTENS University for five years.

With my best wishes,

Fred Gauss

P.S. My last name rhymes with house

I wasn't clear! Fred realized. *I should have written that I have been teaching <u>math</u> at KITTENS University for five years.*

Math is sooooo much easier than English. In algebra, when I wrote a word problem like **Find a number that when you double it you get 16** *the first thing we did was get rid of the English.*

We would write 2x = 16. Super simple. But there are nine ways to make plurals in English.

1. one hat → two hats	– → s
2. one shelf → two shelves	f → ves
3. one mouse → two mice	irregular plurals
4. one sheep → two sheep	no change
5. one guess → two guesses	s → es
6. one berry → two berries	y → ies
7. one stimulus → two stimuli	us → i
8. one larva → two larvae	a → ae
9. one u → two u's	lower case letter → 's

Fred turned on the light. The person who had lived here before him had left a lot of stuff. There was an old computer, some nice pictures on the wall, and a lot of papers.

Fred looked for some lessons plans so that he could find out what the teacher had been teaching. Fred didn't know whether he would be teaching little kids their ABCs or teaching advanced graduate English students how to write novels.

He found no lesson plans.

He looked for student papers. That would tell him what they were studying. He found no student papers.

He looked for English textbooks. That would help him plan tomorrow's lectures. He found some books on how to sew handkerchiefs (silent *d*), on cooking salmon (silent *l*), and a guide (silent *u*) to playing guitars (silent *u*).

Five things went through Fred's mind:

✤ They do mosquito abatement. I'm going to have to do mess abatement in this room as soon as I get the time.

✤ I'm going to call my little place Gauss House.

✤ Which one of the three English teachers who had quit in the last couple of days was the one who lived here? Was it the woman who was expecting a baby soon, the one who was retiring after 42 years of teaching, or the one who had been drafted?

✤ Why is there such a thick layer of dust?

✤ Why are there no lesson plans, student papers, or English books?

The answer was simple, but Fred didn't see it.

Your Turn to Play

1. Make a guess. Which of these statements is true.

Statement A: There are exactly nine different ways to make plurals in English.

Statement B: There has to be a tenth way to make a plural in English. We couldn't stop at just nine ways.

2. Which of these is an example of litotes?

A) Fred's new house is pretty small.

B) Fred's new house is not very clean.

C) Fred's new house had no student papers in it.

3. The word *was* appears five times on the top half of this page. How do you make the plural of a word? Make a guess what the plural of *was* is. Fill in the blank: How many _____ appear on the top half of this page?

...... ANSWERS ......

1. Statement B is true. We couldn't just stop at nine ways to make plurals in English.

If you have 14 mosquitoes and you kill 13 of them, you have one mosquito left.

    10. one mosquito → two mosquitoes   o → oes

        one tomato → two tomatoes

        one potato → two potatoes

        one hero → two heroes

        one tornado → two tornadoes

        one cargo → two cargoes

However, <u>most</u> words ending in *o* become plural by just adding an *s*.

    studio → studios

    portfolio → portfolios

    igloo → igloos

2. B) Fred's new house is not very clean.

Litotes is an understatement with a "not" in it.

3. It's often hard to predict what will be correct in English. We learn to use English properly so that we don't look dum. (Oops. I meant *dumb*.)

I would have guessed that the plural of the word *was* would have been *wases*, but it isn't.

I would have guessed that it might have been *wass*, but it isn't.

The 11th way to make plurals!

    was → was's   *word* → 's   No if's, and's, or but's.

Chapter Five
Searching for Lesson Plans

There was a thick layer of dust because no one had lived in this shack for years. It had been used as a school storage shed. The old computer, the pictures on the wall, the old file cabinets were all things that had been used at the school but were no longer needed.

On the other hand, Fred liked his Gauss House. It was twice as large as his office at the university. It had a nice tree in front of it. It even had a bed—something that he didn't have in his office. For five years he had been sleeping in a sleeping bag underneath his desk.

He was happy. One key to happiness is not demanding that everything be perfect before you can be happy.

The dust was five centimeters thick. If he were back in Kansas, he would have called it two inches. (5 cm almost exactly equals 2 inches.) He wanted to think in metric units because he was not in America.

It was almost 10 p.m. on Tuesday night. He wasn't that sleepy because he had been snoozing when Sylvia had driven him to Dubbo. He suddenly realized what his number one priority was: *I've got to teach English tomorrow!*

He thought *Maybe there are lesson plans and English books at the school.*

The school was right next door. A night light had been left on, but the front door was locked. Fred went around to the back and crawled through a window that had been left open.

At his university in Kansas, everyone knew Fred. He could wander into any building, day or night, without any problem.

But he wasn't in Kansas, he was in Dubbo.

Stop!

Those are **run-on sentences** —two sentences that are smashed together with a comma.

This is called a **comma splice**. Bad, bad, bad. When I, your author, was in high school, one of my teachers insisted that we never write run-on sentences. If an essay contained even one run-on, she would fail the paper.

F

But he wasn't in Kansas. He was in Dubbo. (Every sentence ends with a period, exclamation point, or a question mark. Every sentence begins with a capital letter.)

What Fred didn't know was that he had tripped the burglar alarm, which sent a silent signal to the police department.

While Fred was looking through the school for lesson plans, he was singing to himself, "Don't call Wagga Wagga Wagga." ♪♬

The policeman got off his horse and tapped on the window. Fred came to the front entrance and opened the door.

Each one was doing his job. Fred was getting ready to teach tomorrow. The policeman was responding to what he thought was a burglary.

Fred smiled and said, "Hi!"

The policeman frowned and asked, "Where are your parents?" If Fred had been a teenager or an adult, the question would have been, "What in blazes are you doing here?"

But Fred was a little kid. The policeman thought he was three or four years old.

Without waiting for an answer to his previous question, the policeman asked, "Where is your home? Shouldn't you be in bed?"

"My home for the summer is the house next door."

"Wait a minute. That's the storage shed for the school." The cop thought Fred was just a little kid making up a bunch of stories.

Fred continued, "I'm the new English teacher for this school. I was looking for lesson plans and couldn't find them at my house. So as the old saying goes, '*If at first you don't succeed, try, try again.*' So I headed over here to the school to see what I could find."

He tried again, "Tell me where your real home is."

This was an easier question for Fred than explaining where his parents are. "My regular home is in room 314 of the Math Building at KITTENS University. I have taught math there for five years."

The policeman tried not to laugh. He knew that four-year-olds couldn't have taught university math for five years. Normally, he would have taken this child back home to his parents, but, in this case, he couldn't find out where Fred lived. Instead, he said, "Let's go and see Margie, a social worker for small fry."*

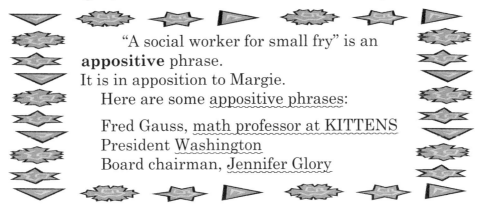

"A social worker for small fry" is an **appositive** phrase.
It is in apposition to Margie.
Here are some appositive phrases:

Fred Gauss, math professor at KITTENS
President Washington
Board chairman, Jennifer Glory

Your Turn to Play

1. Is this a run-on? He ate a Stanthony's combination pizza, the best he had ever tasted.

2. Is this a run-on? He knew the pizza would soon be served, it had been ten minutes since he had ordered it.

---

* When you are a fisherman, you want to catch big fish and not baby fish. Baby fish are called small fry. Small kids are sometimes called small fry.

Young goats are called kids.

We tend to turn animal names into names for children. My father used to call me a silly goose.

· · · · · · · ANSWERS · · · · · · ·

1. He ate a Stanthony's combination pizza, the best he had ever tasted.

   This sentence is okay. It needs no correction. It is not two separate sentences fused together.

   the best he had ever tasted is not a second sentence. It is an appositive phrase.

2. He knew the pizza would soon be served, it had been ten minutes since he had ordered it.

   This is a run-on. There are two sentences with a comma splice. There are three different ways it can be corrected:

✹ Period and a capital. This is the most common way.

   He knew the pizza would soon be served. It had been ten minutes since he had ordered it.

✹ Insert a **conjunction**.* This is also popular.

   He knew the pizza would soon be served because it had been ten minutes since he had ordered it.

✹ Insert a semicolon (;).

   He knew the pizza would soon be served; it had been ten minutes since he had ordered it.

---

* *And, but, or, after, although, as if, because, before, if, though, till, unless, when, where,* and *while* are some common conjunctions.

Chapter Six
In Custody

The policeman asked Fred, "Have you ever ridden on a horse?" Before Fred could answer, he picked Fred up. They headed off to see Margie, a social worker for children.

Fred was curious. He couldn't figure out what Margie needed at this time of night. He knew that he needed some time to prepare for tomorrow's classes.

He was here in Australia to help people, and if the policeman thought he needed to see Margie, he was willing to go along.

The policeman's thoughts were entirely different. All he knew was:

☞ There was this tiny three-year-old who didn't know where his real home was.

☞ The kid had broken into Dubbo School of English for some reason.

☞ The kid liked to tell make-believe stories about how he was a math teacher in Kansas and how he is the new English teacher in Dubbo.

Fred was so happy to think about helping Margie, about teaching English, and about just being alive. He broke into song.

I Teach

Fred Gauss

The policeman sang a second verse to Fred's song. Because he was a man, his voice was an octave lower than Fred's.

I Don't Believe

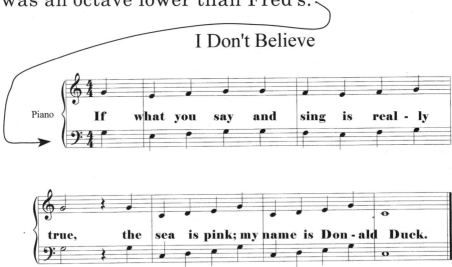

The words of a song are called **lyrics**. (LEER-iks)

> I teach tomorrow English classes here.
> From eight till five I'll make it come alive.
> If what you say and sing is really true,
> The sea is pink; my name is Donald Duck.

This is a poem. (Poems do not have to rhyme.) It has a rhythm, a meter. It is not just a bunch of words on a line.

If what   you sáy   and sing   is réa   lly trúe,

Every line of this poem can be broken into pairs:
da-DUM da-DUM da-DUM da-DUM da-DUM.

The séa   is pínk;   my náme   is Dón   ald Dúck.

Every pair is called an **iambic foot**. (eye-AM-bick)

An iambic foot (da-DUM) is a quiet followed by a loud.

Most of Shakespeare's plays were written in iambic meter. In *Romeo and Juliet:*

But, sóft! what líght through yónder wíndow bréaks?

1. The most common kind of foot in English poetry is iambic.

2. The most common length of a line in English poetry is five iambic feet.

3. da-DUM da-DUM da-DUM da-DUM da-DUM is called **iambic pentameter**. (pen-TAM-a-terr)

(with the *a* like the *a* in alone)

4. *penta* means five.

In geometry this is called a pentagon.

pentathlon = an athletic contest consisting of five different track and field events.

pentatonic scale = a musical scale with five different tones.

Pentateuch = first five books of the Old Testament

pentarchy = a government consisting of five persons. (Much more common is a monarchy = government ruled by a single person.)

Poetry for Adults

Iambic is not the only possible foot. Pentameter is not the only possible length of a line.

Iambic da-DUM	*Dimeter two feet*
Trochaic DUM-da	*Trimeter three feet*
Anapestic da-da-DUM	*Tetrameter four feet*
Dactylic DUM-da-da	*Pentameter five feet*
	Hexameter six feet

Anapestic tetrameter:

/   /   /   /
There are brains, though they moulder, that dream in the tomb.

Your Turn to Play

1. You can mark the **scansion** (SKAN-shun) of a poem by putting in the stress marks (/). When you figure out the rhythm (the meter) of a poem, you are giving the scansion of that poem.

For example, the scansion of one of the most famous lines from Shakespeare's *Twelfth Night*

If music be the food of love, play on

would be:

If mùsic be the fóod of lóve, play ón

Provide the scansion for

Is this a time for smile and sigh,
For songs among the secret trees   (from Christina Rossetti's
                                        "The Convent Theshold.")

With the dew on his brow, and the rust on his mail;
And the tents were all silent, the banners alone
                                        (from George Gordon Byron's
                                        "The Destruction of Sennacherib")

2. Is this a run-on? We know there are eleven ways to make plurals in English, there couldn't be any more.

·······ANSWERS·······

1.   Is this a time for smi/le and si/gh,

                                                          Iambic
    For songs among the secret trees

    With the dew on his brow, and the rust on his mail;

                                                          Anapestic
    And the tents were all silent, the banners alone

2. This is a run-on with a comma splice. We know there are eleven ways to make plurals in English, there couldn't be any more.

Three ways to fix it:

❉ We know there are eleven ways to make plurals. There couldn't be any more.

❉ We know there are eleven ways to make plurals because there couldn't be any more.

❉ We know there are eleven ways to make plurals; there couldn't be any more.

Here's a twelfth way!
For words ending in *x*, *ch*, *sh*, or *z*, add *es*.

    box → boxes
    bench → benches
    crash → crashes
    waltz → waltzes

Chapter Seven
Helping Margie

It was after 10 o'clock at night, and the policeman suddenly realized that he was riding down the street singing "My name is Donald Duck" at the top of his voice.

Fred has that effect on people sometimes; they just get happy and silly.*

He told Fred that they should be a little more quiet so they wouldn't wake up people. Fred switched to humming.

Hum Hum Hum

The policeman was amazed. Usually, when he finds some lost three-year-olds and has to take them back to the police station, they are frightened and crying. In contrast, Fred was having a good time having a horsey ride down the street and going off to help Margie, a social worker for small fry.

---

* I used a semicolon to connect these two sentences. Originally, I wrote Fred has that effect on people sometimes. They just get happy and silly. However, I wanted those two sentences to be more closely connected so I used a semicolon.

When they got to the police station, the policeman lifted Fred off of the horse. He left the horse outside and took Fred down the hallway. There were nine vending machines, four on the left and five on the right. (4 + 5 = 9) This, somehow, felt very familiar to Fred.

Margie's office was at the end of the hallway.

Fred looked at the poster on her door. He thought to himself *That's a weird looking animal. It looks like a rabbit, but there are no rabbits like that in Kansas.*

When Fred read the sign "Child Protective Services," he thought he had figured out why Margie needed help. He knew what protective services meant: protecting things. Night watchmen guard buildings so that thieves[*] won't break in and steal things. Fred imagined that Margie was looking for kids to help guard things. That's why she needed help. Fred was eager to help. (He wasn't *anxious* to help. *Anxious* comes from *anxiety*, which means full of

---

[*] Rule 2 for making plurals: one thief → two thieves.

     f → ves

fear or worried. Fred was looking forward to doing protective work.) He wondered whether he would get a uniform and a badge.*

The policeman knocked on the door and took Fred inside to meet Margie.

She gave Fred a sheet of paper and some crayons to play with while she listened to the policeman's story.

Margie

He whispered (silent h): "This kid broke into the Dubbo School of English. Claimed he was the new English teacher and that he was living in the school shed. You should hear the stories he tells about being a math prof at some university in Kansas. He's a super-nice kid but really into make-believe."

The policeman left, and Margie turned to see what Fred was doing. He had just finished his drawing. He thought that the paper and crayons were part of the job application to work in protective service, so he drew a picture of himself with a policeman's hat and a badge.

I protect

"Hi. I'm Margie," she began. "What is your name?"

"My name is Fred Gauss. G-a-u-s-s." He spelled his last name.

"Do you know where you live?"

_____

* Fred didn't understand what child protective services really meant. He was completely mistaken.

Fred thought that her question was part of the job application. He answered, "In the house right next to the Dubbo School of English. That's where I'm living this summer before I head back to Kansas in the fall. I will be teaching from eight to five on the weekdays, but could work for you on Saturdays. I understand that protecting things is important."

Margie didn't understand what Fred meant by "protecting things."

She asked, "Where are your parents?"

"My mother is in Heaven. I'm not sure where my father is. I haven't seen him for years."

"Who do you live with?"

"Back in Kansas I lived with Kingie. He's an artist."

Time out!

We write an artist, a book, a cat, a dog, an elephant.

The usual guess is that *an* comes before a word that begins with a vowel (*a, e, i, o,* or *u*) and *a* comes before words beginning with a consonant.

That's not quite right.

For example, a hat, an hour, a T, an M.

We don't look at the spelling of a word to determine whether to use *a* or *an*. We look at its sound.

Put *an* before words that begin with a vowel sound.

an A, an E, an F, a G, an H

Your Turn to Play

1. There are over a half million (500,000) words in the English language. The average adult uses about 20,000 of them in everyday speaking.

I can think of only 22 words that do not contain a vowel (*a*, *e*, *i*, *o*, or *u*). Try to name at least one of them before you turn the page and look at my list.

2. A **long u** is a *u* that sounds like *you*. A long u can be written as ū. The word *music* has a long u in it.

It's called a long u because when it is spoken, it takes longer than words with a short u.

Compare *music* with *put*.

Which of these words begin with a long u? *united, utterly, unicorn, used, under, uphill.*

3. Do we use *a* or *an* in front of words that begin with a long u?

```
. . . . . . . ANSWERS . . . . . . .
```

1. I gave you a real good hint when I wrote: Try to name at least one of them before you turn the page and look at my list.

   Try and *my* are two of the 22 words I could think of. The other 20 are: *by, cry, dry, fly, fry, gypsy, hymn, lymph, lynch, Lynn, lynx, myth, ply, pygmy, rhythm, shy, sky, spry, tryst,* and *why.*

2. The words that begin with a long u: ūnited, ūnicorn, and ūsed.

3. Words that begin with a long u get a *a.*

   a united army

   a unicorn

   a used coat

(So there are words that begin with vowels that get an *a* rather than an *an.*)

Long u's get an *a.*

But long a's get an *an.*   an ācorn, an āge

long e's get an *an.*   an ēqual share

long i's get an *an.*   an ĭcy road

long o's get an *an.*   an ōak tree

Chapter Eight
Intake

When Fred explained to Margie that Kingie was five years old and six inches tall, she knew that Fred was just telling tall tales.*

"How is your health?" she asked.

"I'm in the pink." (an idiom meaning my health is good)

"Do you know how much you weigh?"

"Thirty-seven pounds."

She had him stand on a scale. It read 17 kilograms.

---

* *Telling tall tales* means telling stories that are exaggerated and not really true.

To tell a tall tale is an **idiom**. (ID-ee-um) Idioms are phrases that would make no sense if you translated them into another language word-for-word.

Your mother may ask you to *make your bed.* That's an idiom. She doesn't mean for you to get a hammer and nails and go build a bed.

Your father may tell you that if you don't make your bed you will have to *face the music.* That means you will have to suffer the consequences. It

Face the music?

doesn't mean that you'll have to stare at a quarter note.

Fred wrote next to his crayon drawing.

I protect

37 pounds × 0.45 kilograms/lb.

$$\begin{array}{r} 37 \\ \times\ 0.45 \\ \hline 185 \\ \underline{148} \\ 1665 \end{array}$$

$16.65 \doteq 17$ kg

Margie asked, "What does the equal sign with a dot over it mean?" She had never seen that before.

"It means equals after rounding," he explained.

"How old are you? Do you know?"

Fred smiled. That was an easy question. "I'm five."

Another tall tale she thought to herself. *Very few five-year-olds weigh 17 kilograms. That's the average weight for someone who is maybe three years old.* She asked, "When is the last time you ate?"

That was a hard question. He couldn't remember the last time he had eaten. He shrugged his shoulders. "I don't eat a lot."

(litotes) "I'm not very hungry right now." (more litotes)

Margie filled out the official form, which she had to do for each child that she received.

Dubbo Child Protective Services
INTAKE

11 p.m. 4 June

Name of child *Fred Gauss*   ☒male ☐female

Age *uncertain   maybe 3*

Weight *17 kg*

Police report *Officer found him breaking into the Dubbo School of English. Child told the officer he was a professor of mathematics at a university in Kansas.*

Current emotional state *His affect is happy. No signs of fear or crying.*

Time Out!

Some readers may not know what **His affect is happy** means. The words affect and effect have several different meanings.

Verbs (affect and effect):

How did that affect you (a-**FEKT** with the *a* like the *a* in alone) = influence you

We will effect (i-FEKT with the *i* like the *i* in if) a change = to bring about a change

Nouns (affect and effect):

His affect (AF-eck) = his emotional state.
The effect (i-FECT) of an explosion = the results

As an idiom:

In effect I'm lost = basically I don't know where I am.

Margie continued to fill out the form.

Physical state *Appears underweight but physically sound.*
Attempt to contact parents *Can't find them.*
Remarks *He can sleep here tonight on the sofa I have in the office. Tomorrow I'll call families that may be able to provide temporary care for him until we locate his parents.*

Fred noticed a large picture on Margie's wall.

Margie asked him, "Do you have any questions?"

That was the perfect opportunity for Fred. He asked, "I'm curious about those animals. You must like them. Besides this picture, you have a picture of one of them on your front door. Are they Australian rabbits? I've never seen anything like them in Kansas."

Your Turn to Play

1. Fill in each blank space with either *affect* or *effect*.

When the moose entered the room, Kelly's _____ was pure delight. The moose had a great _____ on the conversation in the room. Kelly said, "This moose will _____ great changes in how we live. It will _____ how often I have to vacuum. In _____ I will have to vacuum every two hours to keep things clean."

2. In Chapter 15 of *Life of Fred: Australia,* there was a small essay "What's a Verb?" which explained that verbs are the action words in sentences. Darlene *smiles.* Brides *carry* flowers. Dogs *run* in Kansas. Cars *bring* pizzas.

   Affect and *effect* can be used as verbs. A moose in my bedroom would *affect* my sleeping a lot. I could *effect* a change by asking him to sleep in the living room.

   Your question: Have we ever explained what a noun is?

·······ANSWERS·······

1. When the moose entered the room, Kelly's __affect__ was pure delight. her emotional state

The moose had a great __effect__ on the conversation in the room. the results

Kelly said, "This moose will __effect__ great changes in how we live. create/bring about

It will __affect__ how often I have to vacuum. influence

In __effect__ I will have to vacuum every two hours to keep things clean." essentially/basically an idiom

2. The short answer: no.

The longer answer: We haven't talked about nouns before.

Nouns are persons, places, or things.

Verbs are the action words; nouns are what the verbs play with.

Here are some examples. The **nouns** will be in boldface. The *verbs* in italic.

Fred *sings*.

San Francisco *loves* **fog**.

Add **seven** and **eight**. **You** *get* **15**.

Life without **pizza** *is* hard to *imagine*.

Chapter Nine
Rabbits and Kangaroos

Margie explained to Fred that those are not Australian rabbits. They are kangaroos.

"I think they look cute," Fred said. "They really do look like rabbits with their ears and their big back feet."

Margie laughed. "There are lots of differences between your Kansas rabbits and Australian kangaroos. Some male kangaroos can be two meters (7 feet) tall. Some can jump 30 feet in one hop."

Fred tried to imagine what 30 feet was like. Since he is three feet tall, that would be ten Fred's laid end-to-end.

"Why don't you lie down here on the sofa," Margie suggested. "I've got some work to do at my desk, and you can take a rest." She didn't talk about going to sleep. Most little kids in a new place would resist going to sleep. Margie knew that if she quietly worked at her desk, Fred would be off to the land of Nod in five minutes.

She was right.

She had suggested that he *lie* down. To lie down is to recline.

She didn't say lay down. You *lay* down a pencil. You lay down a backpack. You lay *something* down.

There are two kinds of verbs: transitive and intransitive.

Transitive verbs need an <u>object</u>.

    I set the <u>book</u> down.

    Ask the chicken to lay an <u>egg</u>.

    He hit the <u>baseball</u>.

    Please lay down your <u>fork</u>.

Intransitive verbs do not need an object.

    I sit.

    Fred will lie quietly till dawn.

    Margie works.

    Kangaroos jump.

When you look up a verb in the dictionary, it will tell you whether it is a transitive verb (*v.t.*) or an intransitive verb (*v.i.*).

Some verbs have both transitive and intransitive meanings. If you look up the verb *spoil*, it has a transitive meaning ("the rain spoiled the <u>picnic</u>") and an intransitive meaning ("the pizza toppings spoiled when they were left out overnight").

Three things are happening.
✳ Fred is sleeping on Margie's sofa.
✳ Margie is working at her desk.
✳ Kangaroos are hopping around all over Australia.

Most of the sixty-plus species of kangaroos are nocturnal (knock-TURN-el) (= active at night). Sixty-plus means "at least 60."

If you are ever asked the question, "What animals are seven feet tall and shy?" The answer is some kangaroos.

They are herbivores. They just eat plants.

Fred was dreaming that he would take a kangaroo back with him to Kansas at the end of summer. He would call his kangaroo Hoppa Hoppa. That would remind him of Wagga Wagga.

He wondered why he had never seen any kangaroos in pet stores. Very few people would like to own a seven-foot tall kangaroo, but the different species come in all sizes. Some weigh only one pound.

Fred thought that a pet kangaroo that was about two feet tall would be a lot of fun.

Only one thing stood in Fred's way: the Australian government. They passed a law that said no live kangaroo could be taken out of the country.*

Why did they pass a law that said, "You can't have any of our kangaroos"?

Here are some facts that may help answer that question.

✍ There is a very large population of kangaroos. During the last 25 years the population has never been less than 15,000,000.

✍ The government permits a limited number of people to go and shoot kangaroos. Kangaroo meat is sent to more than 55 countries around the world, including the USA and Europe.

✍ Selling kangaroo meat makes a bunch of money for Australians.

✍ There are many places in the world that kangaroos would be happy to live.

Could it be that the "Environment Protection Act" should have been called the "Economic Protection Act"?

---

* The Environment Protection and Biodiversity Conservation Act. The only basic exception is sending them to zoos in other countries.

Your Turn to Play

1. Which of these verbs are transitive and which are intransitive?

    Fred asked a question.

    Margie phoned.

    Kangaroos hop during the night.

    Kangaroos eat grass.

2. Find the nouns in these two sentences:

    If you light the stove, then we can cook.

    The cook turned off the light and went to bed.

3. Which of these words have a long a (ā)?

    acorn

    alone

    Alice

    across

    make

. . . . **ANSWERS** . . . .

1. Fred asked a question. *Asked* is transitive. *Question* is the object.

Margie phoned. Intransitive.

Kangaroos hop during the night. Intransitive.

Kangaroos eat grass. *Eat* is transitive. *Grass* is the object.

2. The nouns are in **boldface**.

If **you** light the **stove**, then **we** can cook.

The **cook** turned off the **light** and went to **bed**.

Two things to notice:

① Some words can be either verbs or nouns. In the first sentence *light* and *cook* were used as verbs. In the second sentence they were used as nouns.

② Actually, *you* and *we* are not nouns. They are called pronouns. They stand in place of nouns. It would be hard to read: Fred Gauss went to Margie's office. Fred Gauss got tired. Fred Gauss lay (past tense of lie) on Margie's sofa. Fred Gauss fell asleep. Instead, we can substitute *he* for *Fred Gauss* and *her* for *Margie's*.

3. The long a's are in ācorn and māke.

There are at least five different ways to pronounce the letter *a*.

a   as in act, mat, cat   â   as in Mary, air

ā   as in age, acorn   ə   as in alone

ä   as in father, ah

ə is called a schwa. It is an indefinite unstressed vowel sound. It is the sound of *a* in sofa, the *e* in system, the *i* in easily, the *o* in gallop, and the *u* in circus.

Chapter Ten
What We Know

While Fred was sleeping, Margie was busy trying to figure out a nice place where Fred could live. She knew that it wasn't possible for a little kid who was only three or four years old to live all by himself.

small essay
What Some People "Know"

Margie "knew" that Fred was only three or four years old. She was wrong. He is five.

Margie "knew" that no little kid could live by himself. She was wrong about Fred. He had been living by himself since he was six months old. That's the last time he had seen his father. (The whole story is in *Life of Fred: Calculus.*) It *is* true that most kids who are six months old don't know as much math as Fred did. When he was six months old, he was hired to teach lots of math, including calculus, at KITTENS University.

When one of my daughters was really young, she thought that the way you get money is go to an ATM machine. She thought that ATMs gave out free money.

She was wrong.

Some people "know" that animals like dogs, cats, horses, kangaroos, and elephants need to take a drink of water at least once a day or they would get really thirsty. That is not true for kangaroos. They can survive for months without taking a slurp of water.

Every kid "knows" things that are not true. Part of the process of growing up is discovering which things really aren't true. Some kids, especially at night, think there are giant gorilla monsters with pink and blue spots hiding in their closets. When they get older, they find out that they were wrong.

Every adult "knows" things that aren't true. I know that.

end of small essay

Margie had a list of families who had volunteered to be foster parents. They were willing to accept a child into their home temporarily.*

If it were daytime, Margie would have been phoning foster families to locate one that would like to take care of a three-year-old boy. But it was late at night and this little boy was happily sleeping on Margie's office sofa. The phoning could wait till morning.

---

* Being a foster parent means taking care of a child for a limited amount of time. Adopting a child means accepting a child into your family permanently.

It was five minutes after three when Fred's eyes opened. He thought *Oh my! In about five hours my first English class will be starting. I've got to get ready.*

3:05 a.m.

He sat up. Margie wasn't there. (She had gone to the bathroom.) He left her a note.

Dear Margie,

    I have to go and prepare for teaching my English classes. I'll be glad to help you do protecting work on Saturday.

    Thank you for the rest on the sofa.

        Best wishes,
        Fred

When Margie came back, she read his note and exclaimed, "Oh no! He's flown the coop."*

She raced down the hallway past the nine vending machines (four on the left and five on the right). She headed outside. There was no sign of Fred.

She was frantic. You're not supposed to lose the children you are trying to protect.

Meanwhile, Fred was jogging down the street in Dubbo as happy as a clam.** He was thinking about teaching English. His affect was the opposite of Margie's.

He didn't want to go back to his Gauss House right now. He wasn't sleepy. He ran

———————————————————

* To fly the coop means to get away or escape. It is an idiom.

** To be happy as a clam means to be really happy. It is another idiom, but it doesn't seem to make much sense. How can a clam be happy? You never see a clam singing or dancing.

Before the 1830s, the expression used to be, "As happy as a clam at high tide." That made more sense. People dig up clams at the beach, take them home and eat them. They have to do that at low tide. At high tide the happy clam is in the sand and protected by several feet of water.

through one of the main shopping areas of Dubbo. All the stores were closed. The trees were lit by the street lamps.

This is an actual real picture of Dubbo, which was taken on April 8, 2007

Your Turn to Play

1. The small essay in this chapter, the words *know* and *knew* were often in quotation marks.

> Margie "knew" that Fred was only three or four years old.

This is a second use of quotation marks. They are used to indicate something that isn't true. It wasn't true that Fred was only three or four years old.

(The first use of quotation marks is to indicate the exact words that someone has said. Fred asked, "Are those Australian rabbits?")

Classify each of these as either (1) quotes to indicate the exact words spoken or (2) quotes used to indicate something that isn't true.

A. The politician said, "I am honest as Lincoln."

B. This "honest" politician would steal, lie, and cheat.

C. The "current" news is that the computer has just been invented.

D. He is the "king" of the United States.

.... ANSWERS ....

1. A. The politician said, "I am honest as Lincoln." This is a direct quote. These are the exact words that were spoken.

B. This "honest" politician would steal, lie, and cheat. I don't believe that he is honest. *Honest* is being used ironically (opposite to its real meaning).

C. The "current" news is that the computer has just been invented. It's hard to say exactly when the first computer was invented, but in any event, it's not current news.

Computers are sometimes defined as machines that can do a whole math problem involving several steps. This is in contrast to an adding machine or a hand calculator that can do single operations.

In 1944 the International Business Machines Corporation (IBM) worked with H. H. Aiken of Harvard in creating the Automatic Sequence Controlled Calculator. This was perhaps the first computer.

In 1946 the Moore School of Engineering in Philadelphia built the ENIAC. With its 18,000 vacuum tubes, it operated thousands of times faster than the 1944 machine.

D. He is the "king" of the United States. Some politicians may try to act like kings, but they really aren't kings.

This second use of quotation marks is called **scare quotes**, even though they have nothing to do with being scared.

I use scare quotes when I write about how "easy" English is with its dozen ways to make plurals of words.

Have you ever seen people use scare quotes when they are talking? It's a hand gesture known as air quotes or bunny ears.

Chapter Eleven
Early Morning

Fred tried to imagine what might be open at around three in the morning in Dubbo. He wanted to get some real-life examples to use in teaching English.

He knew that very poor teachers just present rules and expect their students to happily memorize the dry material. Fred wanted to liven up his presentations.

It would be really bad if he just wrote on the blackboard the fifteen (!) ways to make plurals in English.

1. one hat → two hats   – → s

2. one shelf → two shelves   f → ves

3. one mouse → two mice   irregular plurals

4. one sheep → two sheep   no change

5. one lens → two lenses   s → es
   except when the noun ends in a silent s
   one corps → two corps
   one chassis → two chassis

6. one berry → two berries   y → ies
   except when the y is proceeded by a vowel
   attorney → attorneys

7. one stimulus → two stimuli   us → i
   except for these four words:
   one campus → two campuses
   one census → two censuses
   one status → two statuses
   one prospectus → two prospectuses

8. one larva → two larvae   a → ae
        except for two words:
        agenda → agendas
        antenna → antennas (if it's a radio)
        antenna → antennae (if it's an insect)

9. one m → two m's   lower case letter → 's

10. one potato → two potatoes   o → oes
        except when the o is proceeded by a vowel
        studio → studios
        cameo → cameos
                and except for two words:
                libretto → librettos or libretti
                virtuoso → virtuosos or vituosi

11. and → and's   *word* → 's

12. ostrich → ostriches   ch → ches
        fox → foxes   x → xes
        brush → brushes   sh → shes
        quartz → quartzes   z → zes

13. crisis → crises   is → es
        axis → axes
        parenthesis → parentheses

14. criterion → criteria   on → ia
        phenomenon → phenomena   on → a

And for people's names and other capitalized names
15.   the Joneses   s, x, ch, sh, or z → es
        the Marches
        the Katzes
        the Maxes
        the Browns   otherwise → s
        the Ashcrofts
        Kansas City → two Kansas Citys (There is a Kansas City, Kansas
                                    and a Kansas City, Missouri.)

And he knew that if he mentioned that the
abbreviation p. 27 (which means page 27) has a

plural pp. 27–40 (which means
pages 27 through 40), his students
would all quit studying English
and become mathematicians.

Please teach me
math instead.

p. → pp.
The 16th way to
make a plural.

    Fred decided that he would just teach the
basic rule: If you want to make a plural, just add
an *s*. Later, he might mention the 15 exceptions
to that rule.

    Right now he faced the question of what to
do as he jogged through the streets of Dubbo at
three in the morning. *What is open?* he
wondered.

    He ran past the Dubbo Library, which is
located on the corner of Macquarie and
Talbragar Streets. It was closed. The sign read:
Monday–Friday 10 a.m.–6 p.m. Saturday 10 a.m.–3 p.m.
and Sunday 11 a.m.–3 p.m.[*]

    He knew that he didn't want to go back to
the police station. He didn't want to go to the
emergency room in the hospital. Those are two
places that are always open all night in any city.

---

[*] If you ever visit Dubbo, you will find that everything
in that paragraph is true.

There is a third place that is open at 3 a.m. in most cities in the world.

Perfect! Fred thought. *I could be a reporter. I could find out the news and then write it up for the paper. That would allow me to practice my English before I start teaching at 8 a.m. today.*

He walked in the front door.

The receptionist was not at her desk. No one visits the building at 3 a.m. Fred walked down the hallway. He came to a giant room full of desks. Fred had seen several newspaper movies and knew this was the room where the reporters worked. He imagined changing his name to Clark Kent.

The room was vacant except for the janitor who was emptying the waste baskets. Fred asked, "Where are all the reporters?"

The janitor smiled. "They're all asleep. They work until the middle of the night. There is very little news happening right now. They submit their stories and go home. Right now, we're getting ready to print the newspaper. The presses will start rolling at 4 a.m."

"What happens until then?"

The janitor pointed down the hallway. "We take all the stories to the proofreading room to correct the English."

Fred dashed down the hallway. This was perfect.

Your Turn to Play

1. Margie didn't know what to do. Her job was to protect kids like Fred. Fred was missing. Margie went bananas.

To "go bananas" is an idiom. It means changing from being calm to getting very excited.

If you were just to literally translate the words into German or Japanese, the foreign reader wouldn't know what it meant. (That's one definition of *idiom*.)

We don't say, "He went apples" or "She went plums." (The story is that this idiom developed from the actions of caged monkeys in a zoo when a keeper arrived with a bunch of bananas.)

Here are some idioms with one word changed in each of them. Can you guess what the correct saying is? (Of course, if you've never heard these idioms, there will be no way to guess the right answer.)

A) My duck is cooked.

B) I escaped by the skin of my mouth.

C) He threw in the broom.

D) He got up on the wrong side of the chair.

. . . . ANSWERS . . . .

1A) My goose is cooked.

That means you have made a terrible error and you are going to endure the consequences.

Where it came from: There's an old story about a goose that laid a golden egg each day. The greedy owner thought he could get a whole bunch of golden eggs if he just killed the goose and cut it open. When he did that, he just got goose guts. His "goose was cooked."

1B) I escaped by the skin of my teeth.

Since there's no skin on your teeth, that means it was a really narrow escape.

Where it came from: In the Book of Job, he says, "I am escaped with the skin of my teeth." (19:20b) Those words were gradually changed to *escaped by the skin of my teeth.*

1C) He threw in the towel.

That means he quit and admitted defeat.

Where it came from: In the old days in boxing, when a fighter was so beaten up that he had no chance of winning, his trainers would throw a towel into the ring to indicate that the fight should be stopped.

1D) He got up on the wrong side of the bed.

That means that the beginning of his day was really rotten. It was starting out horribly.

Where it came from: The old superstition was that the left side of things was the bad side. In some traditions the left sides of beds were shoved up against the wall so that you could only get on the right side.

Chapter Twelve
The Proofreading Room

Fred paused before entering the proofreading room. He wanted to show everyone that he was good at correcting English errors. He wished that he had brought Prof. Eldwood's *Modern Dictionary of the English Language*, 1847. It was 1,973 pages long. He wished he had a red pen to show that he was ready to work.

All he had was a pair of sunglasses. He knocked out the lenses and put them on. He thought that would make him look like someone who likes to read.

Proofreader Fred

There was only one difficulty. Fred forgot that he didn't have ears. He took off his glasses and put them in the garbage can. He thought about singing the ABC song, but that would be juvenile.* Everyone knows their ABCs. That

no ears

---

* JU-və-nl (Recall from Lesson 9: the ə is called a schwa and sounds like the *a* in alone.) Juvenile means either: 1. like a child (the positive meaning) or 2. immature or childish (the negative meaning)

wouldn't show the other proofreaders that he was ready to do real proofreading. Since he knew math, he knew the Greek alphabet. He made up a song with the first five letters.

al - pha   be - ta   gam-ma del-ta ep - si - lon.

He burst into the room singing at the top of his voice.

The four proofreaders in the room had been concentrating on their work. They had a deadline of 4 a.m. when the paper needed to be printed.

Make a guess how many of the proofreaders enjoyed Fred's singing.

Multiple choice:

☐ Zero of them

☐ None of them

☐ Less than one of them

☐ The cardinality* of the empty set { }

All of these choices are correct.

One of them shouted, "Hey kid! We're trying to work here."

———————————

* The cardinality of set is the number of members in the set. The cardinality of {✏, ❀, ❦} is three.

One of them asked, "Where are your parents?"

One of them put her hands over her ears.

One of them picked Fred up, carried him into the hallway, set him down, went back into the proofreading room, and slammed the door.
(That sentence has five verbs.)

Fred would have been much more successful if he had quietly entered the room and asked if he could be allowed to help.

A messenger came with more articles for the newspaper. Fred followed the messenger into the room. Fred was being quiet as a mouse. He put some telephone books on a chair so that he could be tall enough. He took one of the articles and a red pen that was lying* on the table.

He began reading . . .

New Kangaroo Coat Fad
The clothing stores in Dubbo were filled with shoppers that wanted to by the newest coat. Its called the kangaroo coat.

------

* Lying, not laying. Laying takes an object. If the red pen were depositing little drops of ink on the table, then you could say the pen was laying drops of ink.

Lying = reclining.

Fred cringed. He had already spotted three errors. He used his red pen.

New Kangaroo Coat Fad
buy
who
The clothing stores in Dubbo were filled with shoppers that wanted to by the newest coat. Its called the kangaroo coat.

It's

Some notes:

♪#1: We have used gray ink instead of red. Books printed in two colors cost a lot more, and we wanted to keep the price down.

♪#2: *Who* refers to people. *That* refers to things.

♪#3: *By* and *buy* sound alike. They are homonyms (or homophones).

♪#4: *It's* means it is. *Its* is a possessive like *his*.

Stop! I, your reader, have a question. Fred is only five years old. How did he learn all about using English correctly?

The same way that he learned math: he did a lot of reading—reading good books. Reading is one of the fastest ways to learn about math, English, history, chemistry, economics, law, and the right foods to feed your cat.

Going to class takes a lot more time and a lot more money. Some teachers are good and some are bad. Some books are good and some are bad. The difference is that you can't shut teachers and put them back on the shelf.

Read five hours a day—in bed, at the kitchen table, on the living room floor—and you'll learn more than spending seven hours a day in school.

Thank you.

Your Turn to Play

1. It's not fair that Fred should have all the fun proofreading. Here is the rest of the article. There are three errors in each paragraph. Please do not write in this book unless you bought it with your own money.

The new kangaroo coats was created by a french designer named Jean. he designed this new fashion in his garage.

The coat has a pocket in the front, old-fashioned coats have pockets on the sides. Kangaroos carry there babies in a pocket in front. Jean said "This new coat is wonderful."

·······ANSWERS·······

1.

French
Proper names (people,
places, companies)
are capitalized.

were
Make the subject and
verb agree.

The new kangaroo coats(was)created
by a(french)designer named Jean. (he)
designed this new fashion in his garage.

He
Sentences begin with
capital letters.

... in the front. Old-fashioned
coats ...
Run-on sentences with a comma
splice.

The coat has a pocket in the front,
old-fashioned coats have pockets on the
sides. Kangaroos carry(there)babies in
a pocket in front. Jean said "This new
coat is wonderful."

their
There and *their* are
homonyms.

Jean said, "This ...
A comma comes
before a direct quote.

Chapter Thirteen
Pineapple Invasion

Fred had read a lot of books in his life, but he had never done proofreading. He really liked it. He thought *This is just like going on a treasure hunt. I have to search through the article and find the "jewels."* *

---

* This is a use of scare quotes. He didn't mean that the things he found were valuable or good. In fact, he meant just the opposite. He was looking for mistakes.

If Fred were a soldier, he might have compared proofreading with finding and killing the enemy.

If Fred were a gardener, he might compare proofreading to finding weeds and pulling them.

If Fred were . . . **Stop! I, your reader, get the idea. Mr. Author, do you know what the word prolix means?**

Sure, *prolix* means being wordy. Why do you ask?

I guess you can't take a hint. (idiom) **Let me spell it out for you.** (another idiom) **You are prolix.**

But I was just having fun. My best comparison to proofreading is being a dentist with that pointy thing he sticks in your mouth looking for cavities. He's proofreading your teeth.

Do you realize that this footnote is longer than the text on this page!

Oops. I guess you're right. Sometimes, I am a wordy-birdie.

Fred picked up another article.

Pineapple Weed Invades Australia!

Adolpha Moskito has just discovered a pineapple growing out of her granite counter in her kitchen.

Scientists are amazed

Scientists from the local university were shocked. They have called in Dr. Ananas from the International Pest and Weed Agency.

Ananas told our newspaper, "I have never seen a pineapple grow without any soil or water, we will have to make sure this plant doesn't spread. Can you imagine if our highways had millions of pineapples growing on them?"

The only error Fred could find was a run-on sentence with a comma splice in the last paragraph.

There was a companion article.

World Reacts to
Australia's Pineapple Disaster

Words of support have poured into Australia from leaders from around the world.

The president of the Americans United Against Disaster wrote, "We stand with you in your moment of great sorrow and loss."

The president of the Corn Flakes Association wrote, "We stand with you in your moment of great sorrow and loss."

The president of KITTENS University wrote, "We stand with you in your moment of great sorrow and loss."

The secretary to the Detroit League of Manufacturers wrote, "We stand with you in your moment of great sorrow and loss."

In fact, everyone wrote, "We stand with you in your moment of great sorrow and loss."

Fred couldn't find any English errors, but he did find the article very boring. He wondered if everyone copied their words out of the same book.*

Fred suspected that they really didn't mean what they had written. A pineapple growing out of a granite counter is weird, but it certainly isn't a "great sorrow and loss."

---

* Fred was right. They all copied their letters from Prof. Eldwood's *Official Letters for All Occasions*, 1852.

Adolpha Moskito received a special delivery letter.

Ace Dollar Investing
3982 Uptown Street
Honolulu Hawaii

June 5, 2013

Dear Ms. Moskito:

Our investors wood like too buy your pineapple. We are willing to pay you sixty thousand, five hundred twenty-two dollars.

Our representative will be knocking on your door within an hour.

Sincerely Yours,
C. C. Coalback
C. C. Coalback

When Adolpha read the letter, she didn't know what to think. She didn't know whether to sell the pineapple or not.

She yelled to her husband, "Hey, come and read this letter."

He read the letter and laughed. "Some idiot has written this letter. There are three errors in the first paragraph and the closing salutation is incorrect. If this clown wants the pineapple, he can give us $60,522. Just make sure that's he pays in cash and not a check.

"I bought that pineapple for three dollars and put it on the kitchen counter as a gift to you. I can always go and buy another."

Your Turn to Play

1. One of the three errors in the first paragraph of Coalback's letter is his using words to write out $60,522. In general, if a number is greater than ten, use numerals (These are numerals ☞ 0, 1, 2, 3, 4, 5, 6, 7, 8, 9). Use words for numbers less than 11.*

What are the other two errors in the first sentence?

2. What's wrong with the closing salutation?

3. Make a guess why C. C. Coalback wanted to buy that pineapple.

---

* Of course, since this is English, there are zillions of exceptions. For example, use words to begin a sentence: Seven thousand, three hundred sixty-four people flossed their teeth last night.

You *may* use numerals for sums of money that can be written in two or three words: a billion dollars (or $1,000,000,000).

.... ANSWERS ....

1. There are two words that are misspelled.

   Our investors ⟨wood⟩ like ⟨too⟩ buy your pineapple.

   would
   Would and wood
   are homonyms.

   to
   To and too
   are homonyms.

2. Only the first word in a closing salutation should be capitalized.

   Sincerely yours,

3. If Coalback could find a variety of pineapple that could grow anywhere without the need for soil, he could make a fortune growing them.

   For those readers who know about Coalback, you might (correctly) guess that:

   ✓ any check that he wrote would probably be worthless,

   ✓ Ace Dollar Investing doesn't exist,

   ✓ Coalback has never been to Hawaii, and

   ✓ he has never studied English or math or history.
   He did spend one summer studying safe cracking. He paid for the course using a stolen credit card.

Chapter Fourteen
Subject–Verb

Fred was starting to admire those who could do proofreading. There were a lot more details involved in proofreading than in learning math. When Fred taught math, the only things that needed to be memorized were the addition and multiplication tables. There were only 36 multiplication facts from 2 × 2 up to 9 × 9, and his students had five years (kindergarten up through the end of fourth grade) to get them memorized.

Getting the subject and the verb of a sentence to agree is one of the things that he was going to have to teach in about four hours from now.

The hat *is* mine.

The hat and the coat *are* mine.

What could be simpler? Right?

Wrong.

Suppose you have a compound subject with an *or* in it.　　The hat or the coat　?　mine.

The hats or the coats　?　mine.

The hats or the coat　?　mine.

The hat or the coats　?　mine.

𝕿𝖍𝖊 𝕽𝖚𝖑𝖊: With a compound subject using *or*, you only pay attention to the subject closest to the verb.

> The hat or the coat *is* mine.
> The hats or the coats *are* mine.
> The hats or the coat *is* mine.
> The hat or the coats *are* mine.

𝕿𝖍𝖊 𝕽𝖚𝖑𝖊: *Neither . . . nor* work the same way as *or*.

> Neither the coat nor the hats *are* mine. Hats is closest to the verb and it is plural.
> Neither the hats nor the coat *is* mine.

𝕿𝖍𝖊 𝕽𝖚𝖑𝖊: Ignore the garbage that gets in between the subject and the verb.

> The beginning English student who faces all the rules and exceptions is often overwhelmed.

If we shrink down the garbage: The beginning English **student** who faces all the rules and exceptions **is** often overwhelmed.

Time out!

We have frequently mentioned how much harder English is than math. Now it's time to talk about how simple English is.

English is really simple compared with many other languages. Let's look at a simple verb *to play*.

In English:

	singular	plural
first person	I play	we play
second person	you play	you play
third person	he play**s**	they play

The only thing you have to remember is to tack on an *s* for the third person singular.*

In German it is a lot tougher:

	singular	plural
first person	ich spiele	wir spielen
second person	{ du spielst	{ ihr spielt
	{ Sie spielen	{ Sie spielen
third person	er spielt	sie spielen

There are two forms of *you* in German. You use *du* or *ihr* when speaking to close members of your family, to intimate friends, to God, to small

---

* He plays. She plays. It plays. There are three third-person singular pronouns: *he*, *she*, and *it*.

children, and to animals. You use the polite form, *Sie*, in all other cases.

❀   ❀   ❀

It was 4 a.m. on Wednesday, June 5. The five proofreaders had finished their work. The newspaper was ready to be printed. Four of them headed home to their families. Fred sat there. He didn't know what to do with himself.

He wasn't hungry.

No stores or libraries were open.

He had looked in his shack and through the school for lesson plans and hadn't found any.

He didn't have any idea whether he would be teaching little kids their ABCs or lecturing to graduate students about the literary symbolism in the novel *Moby Dick*.

One moment please. I, your reader, have a tiny question. I'm glad this is a book where I can stop you and ask about things.

Were you going to ask about *Moby Dick*?

No. I know that's a story about a nutty sea captain who wants to kill a big white whale named *Moby Dick*.

So you wanted to know about literary symbolism?

No. I know that you can read many great pieces of literature in different ways. A high school student reading Moby Dick will think it is just about some crazy captain who wants to harpoon a particular whale.

A college student reads the same novel at a deeper level: It has nothing to do with fishing. It is all about how hate destroys the person who does the hating.

What did you want to ask about?

What's a graduate student?

Well, why didn't you say so?

Because you kept interrupting!

Sorry.

Apology accepted. Now, would you please tell me what you mean by "graduate student"?

I can't. This is the fifth page of the lesson. I have to put a Your Turn to Play here. I'll answer it in the next lesson.

Your Turn to Play

1. Select the correct verb:

   A) The first words of the novel *Moby Dick* _is/are_ "Call me Ishmael."

   B) Sixteen pizzas and one chocolate cake _is/are_ never mentioned in *Moby Dick*.

C) Neither Ishmael nor any of his shipmates really <u>understand/understands</u> all of the captain's plans.

2. The American Book Review in 2011 listed the "100 Best First Lines from Novels." The first on that list was, "Call me Ishamel," from *Moby Dick,* the story of the great white whale.

Fill in one word: In the previous sentence the words *the story of the great white whale* is an _____ phrase.

3. Three pages ago I gave the **conjugation** of the verb *to play* in the present tense. I didn't mention the word *conjugation* at that time, but that's what you do with verbs. You conjugate verbs.

List the conjugation of *to play* in the past tense. Please don't look at my answer until you have done the work yourself.

. . . . ANSWERS . . . .

1. A) The first words of the novel *Moby Dick* <u>are</u> "Call me Ishmael." Shrinking down the garbage: The first words of the novel *Moby Dick* are "Call me Ishmael."

B) Sixteen pizzas and one chocolate cake <u>are</u> never mentioned in *Moby Dick.* Compound subjects with *and* use a plural verb.

C) Neither Ishmael nor any of his shipmates really <u>understand</u> all of the captain's plans. *Shipmates* is closest to the verb.

2. It is an <u>appositive</u> phrase. (Chapter 5)

3.

	singular	plural
first person	I played	we played
second person	you played	you played
third person	he played	they played

> The past tense is even easier than the present tense.

Chapter Fifteen
College

Fred headed back to his Gauss House. He had been awake all night and figured that at this point three hours of sleep would be the best preparation for the nine hours of teaching that lay ahead of him.

Ahem. Excuse me. Did you forget your promise?

No, I didn't. I just wanted to sure that Fred was tucked in bed and out of trouble before answering your question.

small essay

What Does It Mean to Be a Graduate Student?

First, you graduate from high school. That makes you a high school graduate, but you are not a graduate student!

Then, if you go to college, you are called an undergraduate.

Then, if you complete a four-year program, you graduate from college with a bachelor's degree. You are called a college graduate but not a graduate student.

Then, if you go on for an advanced degree (a master's or a doctorate), you are a graduate student.

end of small essay

I need to say a little more. Fred is sleeping, so we are not missing any action.

Go ahead. It's not 4 a.m. for me, your reader. I won't fall asleep.

Thank you.   *an appositive*

If you are locked into the government school system, you can bet that going through kindergarten and grades one through twelve will take you 13 years.

If you are super-bright, you might be able to talk the administration into allowing you to skip one grade, but that's about the maximum that can be skipped.

If you are not in the government school system, you can go at whatever speed is good for you. If the material is hard, you can spend extra time. If you want to graduate from high school in fewer than 13 years, that can be done.

When you get to college, you will have a lot of freedom to choose:

☆ which teachers you want,

☆ what time of day your classes will be, and

☆ how many classes you will take.

My grades in college were better than my high school grades. I loved the freedom.

I graduated from college in the month I turned 21.
You do the math.

My older daughter graduated when she was 20.

Each person can choose his or her own path in life.

Fred lay in his bed dreaming. (*Lay* is the past tense of *lie*. Right now I lie in bed. Yesterday I lay in bed.)

Have you ever noticed how silly dreams can be? And yet . . . this dream made a little sense. Fred had been thinking hard about what and who he would be teaching.

Then he dreamed about famous first lines in novels. The first line of George Orwell's *1984* novel: It was a bright cold day in April, and the clocks were striking thirteen.

Fred sat up in bed. He suddenly realized that he had not set an alarm clock. Going to bed at a little after four in the morning, he might have slept until ten and missed some of his classes.

He looked at the clock on the wall.

Oh my! Fred thought. *I've got to get up. My first class starts in half an hour.*

He turned on the light and hopped out of bed. There wasn't time to do his morning jog. He brushed his teeth and combed his hair.

In this case, *hair* was singular. His eyes were a little puffy because of his lack of sleep.

He thought of that old saying, "*The early bird gets the worm*," and wondered if in his case, the saying should read, "*The early worm gets eaten.*"

Fred was a little frightened. He didn't know who his students would be, and he had never taught English.

New stuff can be scary. That's only natural. Once you have done something, the second time is much easier.

He wished that Kingie were here with him now to give him a hug before he headed over to the Dubbo School of English. But he wasn't.

So, without a hug, Fred left Gauss House and walked over to the Dubbo School of English. The lights were on. The front door was unlocked. It was ten minutes to eight, but no one was there in the lobby. He walked into the classroom.

7:55

Your Turn to Play

1. Find the silent letters in:

    muscle

    fudge

    autumn

    yolk

three yolks

2. Most verbs in English are **regular**.
To form the past tense, you just add *–ed*.

    fill → filled

    offer → offered

    play → played

    The **irregular verbs** are often the most commonly
used verbs.   sing → sang

    come → came

    begin → began

    try → tried

    make → made

Classify each of these are regular or irregular:

    chew

    do

    email

    draw

3. Conjugate the verb *to run* in
the present and the past tense.

·······ANSWERS·······

1. mus<u>c</u>le
    fu<u>d</u>ge
    autum<u>n</u>
    yo<u>l</u>k

2.   chew → chewed   regular verb
        do → did   irregular verb
        email → emailed   regular verb
        draw → drew   irregular verb

3.   Present tense

	singular	plural
first person	I run	we run
second person	you run	you run
third person	he runs	they run

        Past tense

	singular	plural
first person	I ran	we ran
second person	you ran	you ran
third person	he ran	they ran

    To run is an irregular verb.

Chapter Sixteen
In the Classroom

Twelve sixth graders were quietly sitting and waiting for their new teacher to arrive. They had been told that Professor Fred Gauss was his name.

Some of them had looked on the Internet and had found out that he was the most famous teacher at KITTENS University and that he had won many teaching awards in the five years that he had taught there.

What they didn't know was that he was three feet tall and only five years old.

appositive

When Fred walked in, one of the students, Mike, asked him, "Hi. Are you looking for someone?"

Fred was afraid they were going to ask him the usual questions, such as, "Are you lost?" or "Where are your parents?"

He wasn't looking for *someone*, he was looking for the classroom he was supposed to teach in.

He couldn't speak.

Fred turned red. He had become unsettled.* He turned around and ran back into the lobby. Helen, another of the sixth graders, followed him.

> an appositive phrase

Fred was sitting on the floor in a corner. The combination of a lack of sleep and facing a new situation were a little too much for him.

Fred was in a tight little ball with his knees up near where his ears would be if he had ears.

---

* He was agitated, upset, disconcerted, disquieted, discomposed, shaken, ruffled, and rattled.

You use a **dictionary** to look up the meanings of words you don't know. At my house I do most of my reading at five spots: the dining room table, the recliner, a window seat, my writing room, and in bed. I have five dictionaries, one at each of these spots. When I encounter a word that I don't know, I look it up and also learn to pronounce it. Yesterday, I was reading a sermon, "Is Death Minatory?" You can guess which word I had to look up.

You use a **thesaurus** to look up ideas—not words—and find a range of words and phrases that are associated with that idea. I did that in the first sentence of this footnote.

You could have put him in a grocery bag and still have had room for a carton of eggs.

Helen said, "It's okay. I get scared too sometimes." She gently picked him up and carried him back into the classroom. She was surprised at how light he was.

Math Break

Not needed for this essay

A pint of water weighs about a pound. There are two pints in a quart and four quarts in a gallon. (The metric system is so much easier.) So a gallon of water weighs about eight pounds. So Fred, who weighs 37 pounds, weighs a little more than four gallons of water.

So when you see a gallon of water or milk in the store, that's about a quarter of a Fred.

Helen set Fred on her lap. He was shaking, but only a little bit. She tried to reassure him, "It's okay. When Professor Gauss comes, he will know what to do."

He started crying. He had been under a lot of stress. On Sunday he had volunteered. He lost a day crossing the International Date Line. He had not had much sleep. The school shed where he was staying was a big mess. It was now Wednesday and he missed his home. He didn't know what part of English he was supposed to be teaching. And now he was embarrassed. He thought *How can I tell them I'm supposed to be their teacher? Are they going to laugh at me?*

Mike handed him his handkerchief and said, "It's clean. Blow your nose."

Fred did as he was told. His nose cut a big rip in Mike's handkerchief.

"It's okay, man, I've got another one."

At this point Fred knew that things could not possibly get any worse.

In walked the sheriff of Dubbo. He said, "Excuse me. All of the law enforcement personnel are trying to find a kid who escaped from child protective services a couple of hours ago. If you happen to see him, please give us a call." Stan left.

Cowboy Stan
the Dubbo Sheriff

Fred, who was hiding behind the ripped handkerchief, whispered, "Don't say anything. I'll explain after he's gone."

Helen took Mike's handkerchief off Fred's nose. She waited for Fred to talk.

Fred said, "The Board of Missions asked me to come here to Australia to teach." He then went into all the details of his trip, of Mack meeting him at the airport, of Sylvia driving him from Wagga Wagga to Dubbo, of it getting dark and cold in June, of her tucking him in bed and telling him that he would be teaching English, of his looking for lesson plans, of the nice policeman on horseback who took him to see Margie, of his work at the local newspaper, of his singing his "Alpha, Beta, Gamma, Delta, Epsilon" song, of learning to proofread, of pineapples growing on granite kitchen counters, of. . . ."

"Wait a minute," said Mike. "Are you telling us you are our new teacher?"

Fred swallowed. "Yes."

Your Turn to Play

Fred didn't get a chance to mention his dream about the kangaroo and the clock striking thirteen.

I didn't get a chance to mention how to conjugate a verb in all three **tenses**: present, past, and future.

For example, here is the conjugation of *to stand*.

Present	singular	plural
first person	I stand	we stand
second person	you stand	you stand
third person	he stands	they stand
Past		
first person	I stood	we stood
second person	you stood	you stood
third person	it stood	they stood
Future		
first person	I will stand	we will stand
second person	you will stand	you will stand
third person	she will stand	they will stand

I got tired of using *he* all the time.   **Your question:** Conjugate *to rise*.

.......ANSWERS.......

The conjugation of *to rise* in all three tenses.

Present tense	singular	plural
first person	I rise	we rise
second person	you rise	you rise
third person	she rises	they rise

Past tense		
first person	I rose	we rose
second person	you rose	you rose
third person	it rose	they rose

Future tense		
first person	I will rise	we will rise
second person	you will rise	you will rise
third person	he will rise	they will rise

The word *shall* is sometimes used in place of *will* for emphasis.

We shall overcome.

Here are some FALSE sentences: There are only three tenses in English. There are only four tenses in English. There are only five tenses in English.

Here is a true sentence: The number of tenses in English is evenly divisible by three.

Chapter Seventeen
Begin Teaching

Fred was worried that the sheriff would come back. He wanted to teach all his classes today. He wondered how he could hide and teach at the same time.

He spotted a mop in the corner of the classroom. He took off the handle. The mop made a perfect disguise. (silent u)

Mike laughed and said that his teacher looked like Einstein.

Fred didn't know where to begin teaching. He stood in front of that dozen sixth graders and asked what they had been studying. He didn't know whether he should start by writing A B C D E F G H I J K L M N O P Q R S T U V W X Y Z on the blackboard or by discussing how modern writers have responded to the despair of the twentieth century existentialists.*

---

* Existentialism = the world has no meaning or purpose. "You're on your own, buddy. Tough it out." It's the opposite of what you learn in Sunday school.

Fred asked the class, "Do you have a textbook that you are studying?"

Everyone in the class held up a copy of . . .

Oh no! Fred thought to himself. *They are reading baby books.*

Helen explained, "We don't have a lot of money at this school. (litotes) Our former teacher found 300 copies of this kiddie book in the school shed. All the classes use them."

Fred looked at the cover the book. He figured that he would start there and asked, "Does anyone know why *Ducky, Sings,* and *Opera* are all capitalized?"

Twelve kids raised their hands. Hans said, "All the words of a title are capitalized."

Peter said, "Not every word. Prepositions such as *before, under,* and *with* are not capitalized."

Tom corrected Peter, "Except if the preposition is at the beginning of the title. The first word of a title is always capitalized. The articles, *a*, *an*, and *the*, are only capitalized if they are the first word in the title."

Time Out for Older Readers!

What Tom said is as much as most adults know. English is not quite that simple.

The real rule is that the first <u>and last words</u> of a title are always capitalized, for example, the song "As Time Goes By."

Conjunctions in the middle are not capitalized: *Sense and Sensibility.*

Short prepositions (fewer than, say, five letters) in the middle of a title are not capitalized. In contrast, *Winning Through Intimidation* has a capitalized preposition.

Fred was impressed that the students knew that much.

He asked, "Which word in the title is a verb?"

Twelve hands went up. Mike said, "The word *sings* is a verb."

Peter added, "*Ducky* is third person singular and so the verb is *sings* and not just *sing*."

Tom said, "The verb *to sing* can be both transitive and intransitive. (Chapter 9) When *sing* is transitive, it has an object: He sings a song.

When it is used intransitively, you could write that all day long he sings."

Fred wanted to find out how much this class really knew. "Would someone come to the blackboard and conjugate *to sing* in the present tense?"

Hans dashed to the board and wrote:

Present tense	singular	plural
first person	I sing	we sing
second person	you sing	you sing
third person	Ducky sings	they sing

Fred said, "It's wonderful that there can only be two **numbers** in a language: singular and plural. Some things stay simple."*

Fred was happy to do all this teaching without even having to open the textbook. He could start his teaching by just looking at the cover.

He was feeling better.

I, your reader, get the feeling . . .

Yes.

---

* Fred was wrong. The number in Russian can be singular, plural, or really plural. There are three choices.

Every time, it seems, that things start to look a little normal and happy for Fred, something unexpected happens. It's called foreshadowing in literature. In a film, for example, when the hero has small pain in his tummy in the first minutes of the film, you can bet that somewhere in the middle of the film something serious will be happening to his stomach.

Let me assure you. Fred is just going to ask some students to come up to the blackboard and conjugate *to sing* in the other tenses. They will do it in English—not in Russian. They won't make any mistakes. No police are going to come and take Fred away. Okay? Do you feel better now?

Maybe. Sort of. Kinda. Perhaps.

Your Turn to Play

Proofread this first page of *Ducky Sings Opera*.

(There are three errors in each paragraph. A tenor is a male singer who sings in a high range, usually from the C below middle C to the G above middle C.)

Ducky had always wanted to sing opera. Then one day he read an ad, which said that the opera company was looking for a duck that could sing the tenor part in there new opera. Called "A Duck Sings Opera."

He got a copy of the opera and plaid the lyrics on his piano. He new this was the opera that was meant for him.

He practiced for a hour, then he telephoned. He said "I'm the tenor you are looking for."

. . . . ANSWERS . . . .

an ad that said
that vs. *which* was discussed on pages 67, 68, 71,
72, 83, 84, 89, 90, and 101 in the previous book.

Ducky had always wanted to sing opera. Then one
day he read an ad, which said that the opera company
was looking for a duck that could sing the tenor part in
there new opera. Called "A Duck Sings Opera."

their
spelling

It was called . . .
Not a sentence.

music
wrong word   lyrics = words of a song
See Chapter 6.

played
spelling

He got a copy of the opera and plaid the lyrics on his
piano. He new this was the opera that was meant for
him.

knew
spelling

for an hour. Then he . . .
run-on sentence with a comma splice

an hour
an before words that begin with
a vowel sound   See Chapter 7.

He practiced for a hour, then he telephoned. He said
"I'm the tenor you are looking for."

He said, "I'm the . . .
comma before a direct quote

Chapter Eighteen
Into the Deep

Hans was standing at the blackboard. He had correctly conjugated *to sing* in the present tense.

Fred smiled. He was happy that these sixth graders knew a lot about English.

He said, "The present tense isn't the only tense in English. There are other tenses." Hans and the eleven seated students all nodded in agreement. They knew that already.

He said, "*To sing* is not a regular verb. The past tense isn't *singed*." All the students nodded in agreement. They knew that already.

> *Fred is getting ready to ask some students to come to the blackboard and conjugate* to sing *in the other tenses.*
>
> *Two pages ago I told you this was going to happen.*
>
> *You, my reader, had every right to feel anxious. This is going to be shocking. Please fasten your seatbelt.*

I, your reader, knew it. When you said at the end of Chapter 16 that there weren't just three tenses in English, I knew that I was doomed.

Fred said, "Hans has done the present tense. Is there anyone willing to conjugate the irregular verb *to sing* in the other tenses? Let's have one student for each tense."

It was quiet for a moment.

Then all eleven students stood up and walked to the board.

Wait a minute! At the end of Chapter 16 you said that there aren't just four or five tenses, and you said that the number of tenses was evenly divisible by three.

I did.

I was expecting that there would be six tenses. Are you telling me . . . I'm losing my voice. You said that eleven students stood up and joined Hans at the blackboard. There couldn't be. . . ."

But there are. Here's the math: $1 + 11 = 12$

Three divides evenly into 12. $3\overline{)12}$ with 4 above

Helen did the past tense.

	singular	plural
first person	I sang	we sang
second person	you sang	you sang
third person	Ducky sang	they sang

Tom did the future tense.

	singular	plural
first person	I will sing	we will sing
second person	you will sing	you will sing
third person	he will sing	they will sing.

Okay. I'm dying of curiosity. What else could there be other than present, past, and future? Either something happened in the past, or it is happening right now, or it will happen.

That's true, but that doesn't prevent English from having 12 tenses. Let me continue the story.

Okay.

Peter did the **present progressive tense**.

	singular	plural
1st person	I am singing	we are singing
2nd person	you are singing	you are singing
3rd person	she is singing	they are singing

The *present* part of present progressive indicates that the action is happening right now.

The *progressive* part of present progressive:
- ✏ indicates continuous action
- ✏ emphasizes the action
- ✏ the action is in progress.

Compare **Ducky sings** with **Ducky is singing.**
(present tense)   (present progressive tense)

Ducky is singing almost sounds louder. He's really doing it right now. I want to tell him to be quiet.

In contrast, **Ducky sings** seems to be much more a fact of life. It's something that true like *oil floats on water* is true.
(present tense)

If you tell me **Ducky sings**, my reaction is, "That's weird. I didn't know ducks could sing."

If you tell me **Ducky is singing**, my reaction is, "You're kidding. Ducks can't sing. I want to go and hear this."

Another student did the **past progressive tense**.

	singular	plural
1st person	I was singing	we were singing
2nd person	you were singing	you were singing
3rd person	Ducky was singing	they were singing

Ducky was singing in the shower.

118

Another student did the **future progressive tense**.

	singular	plural
1st person	I will be singing	we will be singing
2nd person	you will be singing	you will be singing
3rd person	Ducky will be singing	they will be singing

Your Turn to Play

1. *Damos un paseo* is an idiom in Spanish. If you use a dictionary and just translate the words, you get *Let's give a walk*. In English we say, "Let's *take* a walk." That's an idiom in English. We really aren't *taking* anything.

In Norwegian is the idiom: *Han er darlig utstyrt i oeverst etasje*. If you run to the dictionary, this will translate as, "He is poorly equipped on the top floor."

Make a guess what *Han er darlig utstyrt i oeverst etasje* really means.

2. Conjugate *to think* in the six tenses that you now know.

> This is one of the world's most famous sculptures.
> Rodin wrote, "What makes my Thinker think is that he thinks not only with his brain, with his knitted brow, his distended nostrils and compressed lips, but with every muscle of his arms, back and legs, with his clenched fists and gripping toes."

Auguste Rodin's
The Thinker, 1880

. . . . . . .ANSWERS . . . .

1. The corresponding idiom in English is, "He is not the sharpest tool in the shed," or "He is three sandwiches short of a picnic."   Translation: He isn't very bright.

2.

Present tense	singular	plural
1st person	I think	we think
2nd person	you think	you think
3rd person	Fred thinks	they think

Past tense	singular	plural
1st person	I thought	we thought
2nd person	you thought	you thought
3rd person	Helen thought	they thought

Future tense	singular	plural
1st person	I will think	we will think
2nd person	you will think	you will think
3rd person	he will think	they will think

Present progressive tense	singular	plural
1st person	I am thinking	we are thinking
2nd person	you are thinking	you are thinking
3rd person	Tom is thinking	they are thinking

Past progressive tense	singular	plural
1st person	I was thinking	we were thinking
2nd person	you were thinking	you were thinking
3rd person	she was thinking	they were thinking

Future progressive tense	singular	plural
1st person	I will be thinking	we will be thinking
2nd person	you will be thinking	you will be thinking
3rd person	it will be thinking	they will be thinking

computers?

Chapter Nineteen
Six More Tenses in Four Pages

Fred had never heard of the present progressive, the past progressive, or the future progressive tenses.

Six of the students had already conjugated *to sing* in six different tenses. The other six were getting ready to conjugate it in six more tenses.

Fred tried to imagine what those other tenses would be. He thought "not only with his brain, with his knitted brow, his distended nostrils and compressed lips, but with every muscle of his arms, back of legs, with his clenched fists and gripping toes." The only difference between Fred and Rodin's thinker is that Fred was wearing clothes.[*]

The Thinker by Stan

After a millionth ($\frac{1}{1,000,000}$) of a second, Fred figured it out.

---

[*] Actually, there is one other difference. Rodin's thinker is six foot seven inches tall *seated!*

As they say in Norway (where they speak Norwegian), Fred is not poorly equipped on the top floor.

Fred thought *If the progressive tense indicates continuous action, then there has to be a tense that indicates the action stops at some point.* It's that simple.

The "stopping" tenses are called **perfect tenses**. (I don't know why; that's just their name.)

> Good use of a semicolon to prevent a run-on.

Look at the first two sentences in *Ducky Sings Opera*: Ducky had always wanted to sing opera. Then one day he read an ad.

Ducky had wanted to sing is in the past perfect tense. It "stopped" when one day he read an ad.

More examples of the past perfect tense: Fred had taught math until he volunteered to teach English. (past perfect)   (past)

We had spent lots of money before the market crashed.

The first sentence of this chapter is in the past perfect: Fred had never heard of the present progressive. But he had once the students went to the blackboard.

The **present perfect** starts in the past and ends now. Ducky has sung in several duck choirs.

C.C. Coalback has been arrested eight times. That takes us up to the present moment. By the time he dies, that number will probably be a lot higher.

When a mother finds her lost child, she might say, "I have looked for you in every aisle of this store." She has found her kid and is no longer looking.

The future perfect describes an action that[*] starts in the future and ends.
Ducky will have made seven phone calls before he is accepted into the opera production.
Fred will have taught at KITTENS University for 60 years before he thinks of retiring.

---

[*] Note that we do not say, "an action, which starts in the future. . . ." *That starts in the future* is essential to the meaning of the sentence; it is not an add-on.

The last three students approached the blackboard. The first three had done present, past, and future.

| past perfect |

The next three had covered present progressive, past progressive, and future progressive.

The next three had presented the present perfect, the past perfect, and the future perfect.

It was obvious—at least to Fred—what the last three have to be.

Present perfect progressive

Ducky has been singing for years.

Past perfect progressive

Ducky had been dancing before he decided to be a singer.

Future perfect progressive

Ducky will have been auditioning for a couple of years before he will finally be accepted.

It was nine o'clock. The sixth graders asked if they could join the ten o'clock class. They were having so much fun that they didn't want to stop.

Fred said yes.

Fourteen eleventh graders came into the room. There were now 26 students, each with a copy of *Ducky Sings Opera*.

Index

To see descriptions of all of the Life of Fred books . . .

FredGauss.com